BREAKOUT BIOGRAPHIES

TIM COOK

Industrial Engineer and CEO of Apple

Amy Hayes

PowerKiDS press

New York

Published in 2018 by The Rosen Publishing Group, Inc.
29 East 21st Street, New York, NY 10010

First Edition

Editor: Elizabeth Krajnik
Book Design: Tanya Dellaccio

Photo Credits: Cover Taylor Hill/Getty Images Entertainment/Getty Images; cover, back cover, pp. 1, 3, 4, 6, 8, 10, 12, 14, 16, 18, 20, 22, 24, 26, 28, 30–32 ninanaina/Shutterstock.com; pp. 5, 13, 23 (bottom) Justin Sullivan/Getty Images News/Getty Images; pp. 7 (bottom), 9 (both) Jeff Haller/The Washington Post/Getty Images; p. 7 (top) Sean Pavone/Shutterstock.com; p. 11 EQRoy/Shutterstock.com; p. 15 (top) David Paul Morris/Getty Images News/Getty Images; pp. 15 (bottom), 17 (bottom) Andrew Burton/Getty Images News/Getty Images; p. 17 (top) Ian Gavan/ Getty Images Entertainment/Getty Images; p. 19 (top) Anton_Ivanov/Shutterstock.com; p. 19 (bottom) Kevork Djansezian/Getty Images News/Getty Images; p. 21 Bloomberg/Bloomberg/ Getty Images; p. 23 (top) Jesse33/Shutterstock.com; p. 25 (top) Drew Angerer/Getty Images News/ Getty Images; p. 25 (bottom) Theo Wargo/Getty Images Entertainment/Getty Images; p. 27 (both) STR/ AFP/Getty Images; p. 29 Stephen Lam/Getty Images News/Getty Images.

Library of Congress Cataloging-in-Publication Data

Names: Hayes, Amy, author.
Title: Tim Cook : industrial engineer and CEO of Apple / Amy Hayes.
Description: New York : PowerKids Press, [2018] | Series: Breakout
   biographies | Includes bibliographical references and index.
Identifiers: LCCN 2017001483| ISBN 9781508160748 (pbk. book) | ISBN
   9781508160755 (6 pack) | ISBN 9781508160779 (library bound book)
Subjects: LCSH: Cook, Timothy D., 1960–Juvenile literature. | Industrial
   engineers–United States–Biography–Juvenile literature. | Apple
   Computer, Inc.–Employees–Biography–Juvenile literature.
Classification: LCC T55.85.C66 H39 2018 | DDC 338.7/61004092 [B] –dc23
LC record available at https://lccn.loc.gov/2017001483

Manufactured in China

CPSIA Compliance Information: Batch Batch #BS17PK: For Further Information contact Rosen Publishing, New York, New York at 1-800-237-9932

CONTENTS

CHANGING THE WORLD

Have you ever wondered what it would be like to change the world? You might think the only people who can make a difference are people like politicians, writers, or doctors. However, some of the people who lead the way into the future don't star in movies or write laws. People can leave their mark on the world in all sorts of ways.

Some pioneers use creativity and hard work to become new captains of industry. People like Henry Ford, who helped make cars cheaper, have shaped the world we live in today. In this age of computers, smartphones, and the Internet, Tim Cook leads the world of **technology** as the **chief executive officer (CEO)** of Apple. How did Cook become the important leader he is today?

As the CEO of Apple, Tim Cook has had a large role in how the world of technology has changed in recent years.

FROM A "LITTLE HOLE IN THE GROUND"

Cook was born in Mobile, Alabama, in 1960. He has an older brother, Gerald, and a younger brother, Michael. His parents, Don and Geraldine, both grew up in **rural** Alabama. In Cook's younger years, the family lived in Pensacola, Florida, and Mobile, Alabama, but they eventually settled down in the small town of Robertsdale, Alabama, when he was 11 years old. His father got a job as a **foreman** helping build and repair ships for the military. His mother worked at a drugstore.

Geraldine Cook described Robertsdale as "just a little hole in the ground" when they first moved there. The farming town was about 5 square miles (12.9 sq km) with only 2,300 residents. Many tourists passed through Robertsdale on their way to and from nearby beaches.

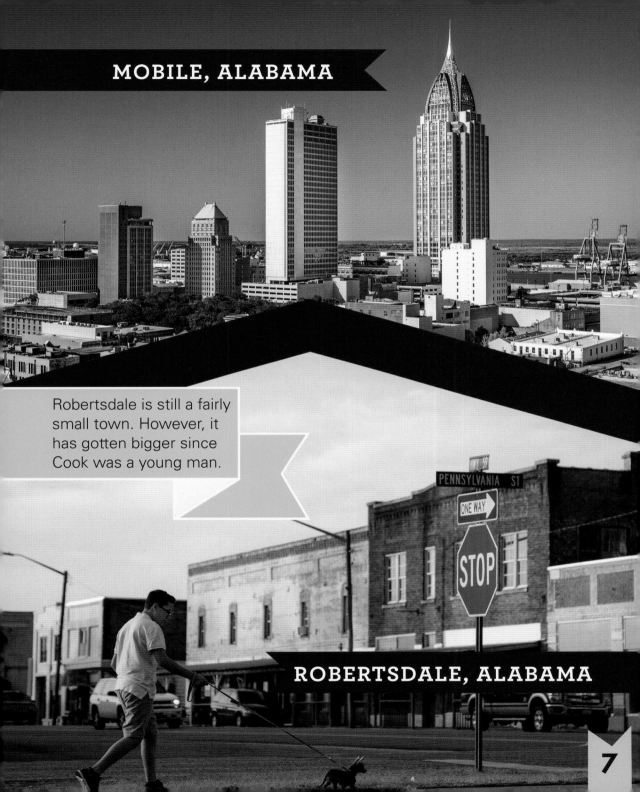

MOBILE, ALABAMA

Robertsdale is still a fairly small town. However, it has gotten bigger since Cook was a young man.

ROBERTSDALE, ALABAMA

A FRIENDLY YOUNG MAN

Many of today's leaders in technology had to work very hard to get where they are today. While attending Robertsdale High School, Cook got good grades, played the trombone in band, and was the business manager on the school's yearbook committee. He was hardworking and organized, but also a friendly person with a magnetic personality.

The Cooks encouraged their children to appreciate a hard day's work. All of the Cook sons worked part-time jobs while attending school. Tim Cook delivered newspapers, worked at a restaurant, and helped his mother at the drugstore. Having a job while maintaining good grades and participating in clubs may not have been easy, but Cook successfully did all three. He graduated second in his high school class and chose to attend his dream school, Auburn University.

TIM COOK'S HIGH SCHOOL

Barbara Davis, Cook's high school math teacher, remembered that "[Tim Cook] was just the kind of person you liked to be around."

TIM COOK

LEARNING EVERY STEP OF THE WAY

At Auburn University, Tim Cook studied industrial engineering. Industrial engineering is the study of making things safely, cheaply, and of the best quality possible. It is an important part of any large business.

Cook went to graduate school at Duke University, where he received a master's degree in business administration from the Fuqua School of Business. There, Cook worked hard to be successful and to learn as much as he could. In 1988, he graduated as a Fuqua Scholar, which means he was in the top 10 percent of his class.

Cook took the skills he learned in college and worked for 12 years at the tech company IBM. He eventually became the leader of the part of the company that builds and **distributes** personal computers.

FUQUA SCHOOL OF BUSINESS

Industrial engineering involves solving puzzles every day. How can you make as many products as possible and make sure they work well? How do you keep everyone in the factories safe? These are examples of important questions industrial engineers have to answer.

THE BEST IN THE BUSINESS

Starting in 1994, Cook spent three years working as a **chief operating officer (COO)** at Intelligent Electronics. He then spent about six months working for Compaq, which was the most successful computer company in the industry at that time. At Compaq, Cook was the vice president of corporate materials, which means that he worked with the company's **inventory**.

In 1998, Apple was not the successful company it is today. iPhones, iPads, and iPods had not been invented yet. Steve Jobs and his friends Steve Wozniak and Ronald Wayne had started Apple Computer in 1976. Over the next 20 years or so, the company experienced success, but by the late 1990s, it was on the brink of **declaring bankruptcy**.

Apple's CEO Steve Jobs left the company in 1985. But in 1997, he returned to Apple with ideas for how to make the company a lot of money.

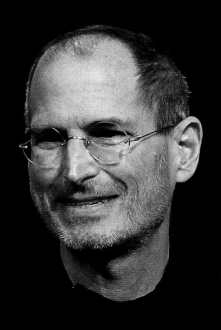

STEVE JOBS

13

A CHANGE OF HEART

Cook's hard work didn't go unnoticed. Steve Jobs decided he wanted Cook to work for Apple. Jobs interviewed Cook in 1998, and Cook thought that he and Jobs would work very well together. Cook felt he could help solve some of Apple's issues. He said in an interview, "I looked at the problems Apple had, and I thought, 'you know, I can make a contribution here.' "

When Tim Cook decided to meet Steve Jobs, he didn't think he would take a job with Apple. However, in that interview, something changed. As Cook described it himself, "It's hard to know why I listened. I'm not even sure I know today. But no more than five minutes into [that] interview with Steve [Jobs], I wanted to throw caution . . . to the wind and join Apple."

Steve Jobs was **adamant** about having Tim Cook join the Apple team. Cook said, "I had gotten a call several times from the search people that [Jobs] had employed." Jobs recognized that Cook would be an **asset** to the company.

A GUT FEELING

An industry leader must have the ability to carefully think things through. Tim Cook weighs the pros and cons of his actions. However, Cook also relies on gut instinct. In his address to the graduating class of Auburn University in 2010, Cook spoke about how much he values **intuition**. "I've discovered it's in facing life's most important decisions that intuition seems the most **indispensable** to getting it right."

A NEW ROLE

Tim Cook started working closely with Steve Jobs as the senior vice president for world operations. It's a big title and it was a big responsibility. His job was to make sure that Apple produced its computers and other technology as **efficiently** as possible, and he quickly became one of the best in the business.

Together, Jobs and Cook came up with three goals to get Apple back on track. These were to decrease inventory, close down warehouses, and cut manufacturing costs.

Cook once compared tech inventory to old dairy products when he said, "You kind of want to manage it like you're in the dairy business. If it gets past its freshness date, you have a problem." This became a new way of operating that helped the company save money.

WHY CUT INVENTORY?

Apple's inventory includes the computers and other devices it makes, as well as the screens, wires, batteries, and everything else the company needs to build its products. While a company needs inventory, too much inventory can take up space in warehouses. This costs a company money. Cook didn't want Apple to pay to keep things stored away.

Companies buy all the parts for their products and have to pay to keep them somewhere. By getting rid of warehouses full of inventory, Cook took a new approach for Apple.

FOCUSING ON PEOPLE

Another new business approach also helped Apple. About the time Cook came on board, Apple started to focus more on personal computers. Less than a year after Cook started, Jobs launched the first iMac, a personal desktop computer. iMacs came in several different colors and were aimed at people who wanted to use the Internet in their home.

After the success of the iMac, the next Apple product to gain a lot of attention was the iPod. The simple design and easy-to-use navigation of this digital music player made it extremely popular. It could hold hundreds of songs and changed the way people thought about portable MP3 players. Apple focused more and more on products that appealed to the consumer, and the company made big waves.

The "i" in iMac stands for Internet. It also stands for the personal and individual nature of Apple's products.

A TURNING POINT

As a young boy, Cook witnessed a terrible event. In a speech in 2003, he spoke about seeing people burning a cross in front of an African American family's home near his home in Alabama. People wearing white robes and hoods—members of the hate group the Ku Klux Klan—were shouting racist things. Cook said this moment changed his life and made him focus on the importance of human rights and equality.

FRIENDSHIP
BEYOND BUSINESS

As Apple continued to become more successful, a strong bond formed between the sometimes difficult Steve Jobs and the calm Tim Cook. Cook's pleasant personality was an important part of steering the company in the right direction, and Jobs valued Cook's vision and hard work.

In 2004, Jobs had to leave Apple for a while to deal with health issues and Cook stepped in as substitute CEO. Steve Jobs returned, but only a few years later he suffered more health problems and again asked Cook to step in. In 2011, it was clear that Jobs was not going to get better. He personally suggested Cook as the new CEO of Apple, and the board of directors accepted Cook for the position on August 24, 2011.

Steve Jobs died on October 5, 2011. Cook was very sad to lose his coworker and friend. Apple's board of directors was certain that Cook was the best man to help Apple continue to grow.

21

STANDING UP FOR WHAT YOU BELIEVE IN

Cook worked hard to bring Apple the biggest profits it had ever seen. He handled his new role well, making Apple stronger despite the loss of Steve Jobs. However, he soon had to face one of his biggest challenges.

In February 2016, the FBI asked Cook and Apple to unlock an iPhone that belonged to attackers who killed 14 people in San Bernadino, California, in December 2015. They wanted any information on the phone. A judge ordered Apple to do it. Cook understood that unlocking the phone would help the FBI, but it went against his belief that people have a right to privacy. He worried that this would make it easier for the government to steal information stored on peoples' phones. He stuck by his beliefs and refused to help.

President Barack Obama invited Cook to speak at a cybersecurity conference at Stanford University on February 13, 2015. Cook talked about the ways he wants to protect Apple's customers and keep their information safe.

THE RIGHT TO PRIVACY

The Fourth Amendment to the U.S. Constitution protects people from unreasonable searches, including phone searches. In the San Bernadino shooting case, the search would have been reasonable. However, **surveillance** in the United States has become a huge issue, especially since the Patriot Act was passed in 2001. Some people think the act weakened the Fourth Amendment. Cook was worried that unlocking the phone would be the first step down a slippery slope towards the government watching what people do on all Apple devices.

THE WHITE HOUSE
UMMIT ON CYBERSECURIT
ND CONSUMER PROTECTIO

WH.GOV

SE
RSECURIT
OTECTIO

SUMMIT
AND CO

23

COMING OUT TO THE WORLD

Tim Cook values both privacy and human rights. For a while, privacy was the most important thing to him, and he did not talk much about himself. Then he decided that he needed to do something to encourage others to be themselves. Cook came out to the world as gay in a letter published in 2014 in *Bloomberg Business Week*.

He wrote, "I'm proud to be gay, and I consider being gay among the greatest gifts God has given me." He said that being gay helps him understand the struggles of others. When asked later why he came out, he said, "It became so clear to me that kids were getting bullied . . . and that I needed to do something."

Since Cook became CEO of Apple, his life has been in the spotlight. Although he still values his privacy, he advocates for equal rights, especially for members of the gay community.

RIPPLE OF HOPE

Tim Cook is dedicated to making the world a better place. In 2015, Cook was one of four recipients of the Robert F. Kennedy Human Rights Center Ripple of Hope Award. This honor is given to those who are dedicated to social change. According to the center, the recipients of this award reflect Kennedy's desire for equality, justice, and basic human rights, and his belief that everyone should try to "make gentle the life of this world."

ISSUES IN
OVERSEAS FACTORIES

It's part of Cook's job to make sure the employees who make Apple products are safe and treated with respect. In the United States, there are many laws about this. However, Apple works with other companies across the world that don't always treat their employees well.

In 2010, there were reports that one of the Chinese companies Apple worked with was treating its workers badly. Apple looked into the conditions at the factory to see how they could be improved. In 2012, a newspaper reported there were still problems and that workers were forced to work too many hours. Apple worked to fix these problems. They checked factories and tried to make sure that companies followed the rules. By 2016, at least one news source reported that conditions had gotten better.

Apple has strict rules to prevent factory employees from working too many hours. At one facility, workers must swipe an ID badge that keeps track of how many hours they work.

WHAT IS A SWEATSHOP?

When people think about poor working conditions, a word that often comes up is "sweatshop." A sweatshop is a workplace that has long hours, pays very little, and is unsafe. According to the U.S. General Accounting Office, a sweatshop is a workplace that breaks two or more state or national labor laws.

LOOKING FORWARD

Cook has been a successful leader in the technology industry. He came to Apple when it was struggling. He helped to change the focus from computers for businesses to computers for people to use in their homes. With the success of the iPhone and iPad, Cook's work has changed the world.

During his first five years as CEO, Cook helped launch the Apple Watch and saw Apple grow and make more money than ever before. But Cook's legacy is more than just money or success. He has donated to charitable causes and voiced his opinions on human rights and privacy. With hard work, dedication, and a level-headed approach, Cook strives to live in a world he believes in, day after day.

With hard work, you too might become the head of a company someday!

TIMELINE

November 1, 1960 — Tim Cook is born.

1978 — Cook graduates high school second in his class.

1982 — Cook graduates from Auburn University with a degree in industrial engineering.

1988 — Cook graduates with an MBA from Duke University. He is named a Fuqua Scholar.

1994 — Cook becomes COO in the reseller division of Intelligent Electronics.

1997 — Cook becomes vice president of corporate materials at Compaq.

1998 — Cook joins Apple as a senior vice president.

2002 — Cook is promoted to executive vice president of worldwide sales and operations.

2004 — Cook acts as temporary CEO during Steve Jobs's health issues.

2007 — Cook becomes COO of Apple.

2009 — Jobs takes leave of absence from Apple. Cook acts as temporary CEO.

2011 — Jobs dies of cancer. Cook becomes CEO of Apple.

2014 — Cook comes out as gay to the public.

2015 — Cook speaks about Apple's belief in the right to privacy and security at the White House Summit on Cybersecurity and Consumer Protection.

2015 — Cook receives the Visibility Award from the Human Rights Campaign.

GLOSSARY

adamant: Unshakable, immovable.

asset: A valuable person or thing.

chief executive officer (CEO): The person who has the most authority in an organization.

chief operating officer (COO): The person who is responsible for the daily operation of an organization.

declare bankruptcy: To begin a legal proceeding involving a person or business that is unable to repay debts.

distribute: To share, sell, or otherwise spread something out.

efficient: Capable of producing desired results without wasting materials, time, or energy.

foreman: A worker who is in charge of other workers.

indispensable: Extremely important and necessary.

intuition: A feeling that guides a person to act a certain way even if they don't fully understand why.

inventory: All the goods and property that a company uses to make its products.

rural: Relating to the country.

surveillance: The act of watching someone or something closely.

technology: The industry that deals with electronics and computers or the use of science in solving problems and the

INDEX

WEBSITES

Due to the changing nature of Internet links, PowerKids Press has developed an online list of websites related to the subject of this book. This site is updated regularly. Please use this link to access the list:
www.powerkidslinks.com/bbios/cook